Streets & San

poems by

John S. O'Connor

Finishing Line Press
Georgetown, Kentucky

Streets & San

Copyright © 2025 by John S. O'Connor
ISBN 979-8-89990-221-5 First Edition
All rights reserved under International and Pan-American Copyright Conventions. No part of this book may be reproduced in any manner whatsoever without written permission from the publisher, except in the case of brief quotations embodied in critical articles and reviews.

Publisher: Leah Huete de Maines
Editor: Christen Kincaid
Cover Art: Tom Lau
Author Photo: Eleni O'Connor
Cover Design: Tom Lau and Eleni O'Connor

Order online: www.finishinglinepress.com
also available on amazon.com

Author inquiries and mail orders:
Finishing Line Press
PO Box 1626
Georgetown, Kentucky 40324
USA

Contents

I. worlds/beyond/the world

On Top of the World 1
Sun Poisoning 2
Refrain 6
Names 7
Hubbard's Cave 8
Immigrant 10
Streets & San 11
Haiku (I) 12
Halfway Up the Stairs 13
Dipso Facto 14
Sweetness 16
Urbs in Horto 18
Guzzle 19
Dredger 20
Ghost 21
Skitching 23

II. worlds/within/the words

Eradication: Radical Fairy Tale #1 29
Sanitation 31
Zeno 32
Adult Literacy 33
Haiku (II) 34
Mermaid 35
Goldfish 36

Tomcat 37

Motley 38

Hunky Dorey 39

After Thought Autumn 40

III. worlds/within/the world

Production Notes for *February: The Movie* 43

Hopscotch 45

Carnival 46

Untidaled 48

Time 52

Midlife 53

Night Meds 54

Assisted Living 55

A Young Poet Responds to Robert Bly 57

Ode to Vivian Maier 58

Haiku (III) 61

Reflection 62

Communication Disorder: Blanche 63

Communication Disorder: Forcefield 64

Pinners 65

A Walk in the Woods with My Daughter 66

for Eleni, Alison, and Ted with all my love

There are more streets in heaven and earth than are dreamed of in your philosophy.

—Machado de Assis

I.

worlds/beyond/the world

On Top of the World:
Photo of My Father, The Empire State Building, 1957

Just out of the frame,
I can almost hear the Texan
Who lifted off his 10-gallon hat
And said, "From the great state
Of Texas, I welcome you to
The U-nited States of America."
And, I can almost taste the two-inch
Thick steak you ate in the Knickerbocker
Hotel down below, the one you compared
all future meals to, the one dripping
With blood and hope.

Half King Kong, half-Cary Grant,
With shoulders wide as 34th St.,
You lean casually against the railing
Of the observation deck,
Hair slicked back,
Rumpled grey flannels.

Tiny next to you, Mom clutches
Her purse to her side. She's heard
Stories about New Yorkers.
Even in black and white,
Her movie star make-up glows:
She knows you'll marry her within a year.

Ten years after your death, you still stand
Front and center in the gilded frame on top
Of Mom's dresser. Nothing has changed.
Your possessions survive you: soiled
Work clothes; torn boxers; empty bottles
Of Royal Copenhagen cologne; tobacco
Ash in a half-filled pipe; and, next to the photo
A bud vase with tiny Irish and American
Flags crossed at the stems.

Sun Poisoning

Cauldron of August bubbling

Over, King and Kennedy, gone.

The west side—the world—in flames.

What's real? The facts: It was 1968.

I was four years old. I'd been

Playing in Columbus Park

With my best friend, Skookie, a black

Boy whose real name was Benjamin

Moore. Cars were overturned. The sun

was liquid, molten. Sunspots

like tangerines danced before my eyes.

I was burning up as if tse-tse-stricken

When I fell unconscious, near the lagoon

On Jackson Blvd. Everything went black.

I should have died they said, but I was saved

By a black man's Cadillac:

Leon the Rib King's, to be exact. I lay

In the back of his royal red sedan,

A little rajah, *red as hot sauce,* or

White as a slice of Wonder

Bread (depending on the teller),

Breathing in the breathy air-

Conditioning until they plopped

Me into an ice bath at Cook County

Hospital. Did my father cry

When I shrieked and shivered?

      Sometimes I yearn for

Those fevered dreams of delirium—

102, 104, 106 … the story changes

Only by degrees—the mosquito netting

Covering my crib, arm and leg restraints

To keep me from thrashing while

Sunspots the size of mangos popped

All around me, my dreams

Turning every shade—magenta, fuscia—

Until the fever broke.

Did the doctor really diagnose

"Sun poisoning"? Were we so primitive

Then?

      White flight they called it:

Don't get too close!

            My father said

We were the last white family to leave

The west side, said we had to leave

the "jungle," said he had a plan

To save us, said everything went black.

And I never saw my friend Skookie again.

Not even Benjamin Moore (whose real name

Was Black Boy) could offer a brighter palette

Than the black and white thinking that

Didn't allow for dreaming in color.

        God, I hated my father then,

And I burn with shame as I write this

Now. What did I know? What do I know?

I was playing with my best friend until

I fell, sun-spots big as grapefruits danced

Before my eyes and dizzied me.

I was saved by a black man's Cadillac,

A man whose license plate read RIB KING,

A man I never thanked.

What's real? Look, this is all I know:

I was four years old and the world—my brain—

Was on fire. Bubbling lava lamp of memory,

What can we see through the scalding caul of recall?

Refrain

Inflammable means "flammable," like my memory
Burns, returns to that fire on the Westside of Chicago,
Where I lived till I was five. I still can't put it out
Of my mind: the giant puffs of black smoke,
And the reckless axes of the firemen, and my father
Carrying me from my bed. I can't help
But remember the way *refrain* means "to hold back";
"A repeated verse."

Across the street, we stand on the curb and watch
The flames consume the only home I'd ever known,
Holding hands like a paper chain
Family—torn apart, connected—
The way *cleave* means "to split with an axe";
"to cling to."

Names

My father worked construction,
Wore a "uniform" of dark flannels
So the dirt wouldn't show.
He put up those green street lamps,
With yellow domes of light
Strong enough to read under,
Though he never learned to read.
My father left school when he was eight
(His father died and he needed to work).
He dug peat in the bogs, ten hours a day.
"John" sounds like bog, a one-syllable,
Dull thud of a name, like a black key
On a piano, worn thin over time.

My older brother was "John"
For three days until my father
Changed the birth certificate.
Now he's Mike for my father
And for my father's father.
I was named for my mother's father,
A man I never met.

John: four letters, four parts to Ireland,
Four angels answered my nighttime prayers:
One at the head, two at the feet,
And one to guard me while I'd sleep.

Once, in French class,
We had the chance
To take a new name.
I chose Napoleon—
The conqueror, not the creampuff.
"Now there's a man," I thought,
"Who really knew his history."

Hubbard's Cave, I-94

In the rearview mirror

Dad stares straight ahead,

his Brut aftershave and whiskey

breath staling the air, his hands

strangling the steering wheel.

Even now I feel the pinch

and itch of starchy Easter

clothes, the four of us

squeezed into the back

of a rusty Chevy Impala

on our way to the Irish mass

at Old St. Pat's where the import

priest with the holy brogue

talks more about the IRA

than he does the Resurrection.

On the Hubbard St. bridge,

Just before the tunnel, a Metra ad:

Easy Come, Easy Go. Below,

an elbow of shadow. Entering

the mouth, Mom homilizes:

Your dad built this cave,

dug the trenches, paved the walls,

Installed the lights—fluorescent

yellow guidelights

striating the view

outside windows so dark

you can see yourself.

Immigrant

(a Golden Shovel poem, by Carl Sandburg)

Most nights Dad'd be down
At The Six Penny Bit, wedged between
Shot glasses, a forest of flannel, and the
World's saddest jukebox. Leaning against the far walls,
A small circle of
Followers mingling their shadows
Into his circle of darkness where
He'd sit like a *seanchai,* the
Tribal storyteller, with his rusty iron
Tongue, an illiterate man, expounding the laws
Of Immigrant Life, insist-
ing discrimination against the
Irish was different, that famine hunger
Was hungrier, the fist-thick brogues joining their voices
In agreement, their leader, haloed in cigarette glow, rising to mock-
Heroic exposulation. This was the only place where the man with the
Second grade education could ply these stories, as worn
As the grooves of the ancient 45s dropping on the juke box: another waif, airing
His grievances into a glass. How hard for the poor to live like men.

The night of his wake, I walked around the funeral home with
His Mass card in my hand. *Grant me the*
Serenity to accept the things I cannot change… hunched
Under the sodium-vapor streetlights he installed, and
Read the prayer he chose though he never learned to read. How humble
And frail he looked in the casket: "Big Mike" with the broad
        shoulders,
The man of smashed furniture-violence, who couldn't throw
Punches at the world, so he saved his anger for home, his wife and kids running
for their
lives, ducking the buckle of the work pants belt and the derisive laughter
Of neighbors. It's taken nearly 20 years for our stories to modulate into
Legend, our uneasy memories into tearless toil.

Streets & San

I never saw my father cry,
Not even in his cancer-crippled final years
When I held his shrunken pink fingers
And whispered goodbye in his good ear,
        the North Sea raged in his blue-grey eyes.

I never heard my father sing,
Not church choir hymns,
Not radio, jukebox, nothing,
But I'm told that after a few at the pub,
        there was no stopping him.

I never saw my father work,
But in my mind's eye, I see him now
Aloft in a blue Streets & San truck
Cherry picker basket, fixing a street lamp
        silhouetted by falling snow.

Haiku (I)

too drunk to stand
the constant gurgle
of the fish tank

                                                      intervention
                                                      my hands
                                                      shake too

Halfway Up the Stairs

I used to linger here
to listen to the grownups
downstairs, their loud
shouts and passionate
laughter. Once, when my father
stumbled home late,
I followed him up the stairs.
When he reached the creaking
stair, he teetered and wobbled,
and for the first time
I felt his whole weight,
weight I could not support,
and I knew if I didn't move
quickly he would take me
down with him.

Dipso Facto

You hear the Montego jerking and braking wildly outside, the incessant muttering, the sound of construction boots up the front stairs, and the door slamming open, smashing against the writing desk on which no one ever wrote.

And the screaming. *Are you awake?* You don't answer, of course, but that almost never matters. The best you can hope for is that it is someone else's turn.

Your mother's, for example. *You've broken my heart for the last time,* or your brother's *You fucking punk. I wish you were never born.*

But some nights you don't get so lucky: He'll say in the super-calm voice he uses when he tries to persuade himself he's not plastered. *I thought you might be able to make something of yourself, but look at you. You're nothing.* Listen and nod, your face as blank as a nurse's uniform; agreeing helps him go to sleep faster. Make him some food or get him another drink. It does no good to argue.

The goal here is silence and a few more hours of sleep. Help him untie the laces on those boots. Try to move things along to the sofa or upstairs. If you can just get him to lie down, he'll fall asleep faster. Agree with everything. Put on Channel 9. Late night laugh tracks soothe. Mom is curled up on the edge of the bed. Her side. There's no way she's sleeping, but let her pretend. One day you'll read Pessoa: *Life would be unbearable if we made ourselves conscious of it.*

In the morning, it's all up to you. Mom has gone to work early. Before you get yourself to school you've got to get *him* to work. Speak softly at first and only gradually increase the volume. Start with a cold compress. In the sock drawer, find the smelling salts he brings with him to weekend bar fights. It looks like a tiny jar of horseradish. He'll choke himself awake if you wave it under his nose two or three times. The TV is still on. It's Ray Rayner now, and Garfield Goose. Tickle his feet as a last resort. Sometimes this makes him convulse to the floor. Get out of the way.

Lay out his clothes. It'll look like a person on mom's side. Dark flannels—a fresh dago tee, a pair of thick woolen socks. Transfer yesterday's pockets over: a pack of Marlboros, loose change, a nail clipper, a handkerchief, and a souvenir lighter from a local casino.

While he's Barbasol and Bryl-creaming in the bathroom, make the call. Use your new voice, your deepest voice. Say, *This is Mike. My car's acting up again. I'm going to be about a half hour late.* The dispatch secretary probably knows, but she says, *See you soon sweetie. Get here when you can.*

Mom has left a fry in the pan—a couple sausages, eggs that were flipped at least an hour ago. Heat them up. When he comes down, he'll ask if she made it. Insist it is your own creation. Two fresh pieces of toast make the whole meal seem fresh.

Do not stare while he is eating. Hand him his thermos and brown bag lunch, your face as blank as a box of Kleenex. Do not follow him to the door. He'll start to say, "Listen about last night…" but don't make him finish that sentence. Say, *Have a great day* in a voice full of sunshine and hope.

Now get yourself ready for school, dickwad. You've got a test on the Civil War in an hour that's worth like a hundred points.

Sweetness

I came of age in the shadow
Of a pair of lips, giant throbbing
Red neon Magi-kist lips,
Smooching the crotch,
The cement-soutured seams
Of the Kennedy and Edens
Expressways. Remember
When the girls turned
Curvy and tackle turned
To one-hand touch? Remember
All those football games
In the narrow alleys
Behind the factories? Listen:
My subconscious is bleeding
On the cracked cement—
And necessity is a mother.
Until the streetlights came on,
We stood over phantom center
And ran our paltry playbooks…
Go long!—I'm thinking of 1976,
The year Walter became Sweetness.
We huddled in dumb wonder,
Contemplating the metaphysics
Of high-jumping an invisible plane.

When the lips collapsed,
Dynamited by the pre-fab SELF-
STORAGE facility, you said
It was another canker scar
On a bankrupt culture,
A naked sign of a vacant
Imagination. You can't have
Everything: you'd have nowhere
To put it. Tonight, I am driving
Against traffic and the night air
Is gasoline sweet. At the merge
Where the lips once blinked
Alive, I feel myself glide past
The membrane of memory

While the evening light leaps
From imperfect into preterite.

Urbs in Horto: Chicago Cartogrpahy

State and Madison, Madison, State—that is all
Ye know on earth and all ye need to know.

Guzzle

> *"The piano has been drinking, not me."*
> —Tom Waits

Your father didn't smash your stereo
into pieces last night. His alcoholism did.

Your father didn't hurl the fridge down
the steps into the back yard. The bottle did.

Your father didn't crash his car into the bus stop
near the hospital. His genetic predisposition did.

Your father didn't hit you with the broom
or belt. His inability to curb his urges did.

Your father didn't beat your brother bloody
all those nights in our tiny room. His disease did.

Your father didn't soil himself in bed again
and ask for help getting clean. His biochemistry did.

Your father never said, "You are the biggest
disappointment in a life full of disappointment.
I wish you had never been born." His illness did.

John, you are 45 years old. When will you ever
Be ready to forgive? I forgive his alcoholism.

Dredger

Even for a big man, Dad's casket
was surprisingly heavy. Mike thought
my *not* crying was a mask, said get a grip
with gloved hands. We held fast to the brass
Bells ringing the recessional. Dad was once
Pinned under a bottom dredger in the North
Sea, I'm told, writhing blindly in the ocean murk.
I mean why, in this rain, would anyone write
Off reincarnation? Just how many St. Joseph
Statues are buried in suburban back yards?
As a child I kept a journal of insect sightings:
backswimmers, coffin moths, praying mantises.
We once lived near a religious store that sold
Candles for Every Occasion: tiny votives, altar-
sized Easter candles; some scented, opaque,
a few always glowing in ghostly demonstration.
Ireland was the site of our only family vacation.
I wore a rugby shirt striped with green and gold.
When we landed in Shannon, mom said, "Johnny
Cash was right: there really are 40 shades of green."
By August this wispy grass will dry out, double over.
Overhead, the disappearing drone of the twin engine.
Why do I still close my eyes at the top of Ferris wheels?
"This is the season of endings and renewals," the priest
sermonized, his squinting eyes glinting like scythes.

Ghost

I suppose it's possible
I brought it upon myself
by going back

                                          to the Irish

American Heritage Center
my father thirty years gone
and far from my mind

                                          quiet at last

when the Dublin lady asked
if I'd ever seen my father's ghost
as he appeared to her one year

                                          after he died

bundled in layers of winter
clothes sitting on his porch
haloed in lamp glow this

                                          hindsight phantom

revenant shade
my sister also saw
Dad taking a postmortem

                                          stroll in the Loop

is it time for confession
I've never pictured him
shivering with the cold

                                          where he is now

looking straight at me that lady
from Dublin said she saw him
that night clear as day

                                    might it have been

my brother who like my father
is long dead and buried
or perhaps I was the man under

                                    all those layers

that lie and lie beneath
the search for self
definition revision

                                    revelation

look I want to be real
here I've seen him too
in the foggy shaving mirror

                                    the odd morning

or when I find myself
raising my voice the specter
of him howling haunting

                                    the empty night

Skitching

Tonight we hide

      behind parked cars—

(black coats, ski masks

      and Sunday shoes)

On Sunnyside,

      a dead end street

Darkened by car

      exhaust and night-

Shadow, sliding

      on ice, ready

To skitch. As soon

      as I see STOP

sign brake lights glow

      I'm off, gliding,

Shuffle-skating,

      To the stopped car,

Curling my bare

      fingers around

the rusty lip

      of the bumper:

invisible

    in the blind spot,

beneath the rear-

    view mirror; smell

of chrome mugging

    the air. (I've heard

stories, of course,

    of lost riders

crushed underneath

    tires wrapped in snow

chains, kids who've slipped

    into absence

between chassis

    and silhouette.

But this is no

    time to think of

urban legends,

    fallen souls in

the art of skitch).

    Riding the crown

The rise of the

        road, between the

pot hole-strewn grooves

        of ice-crusted

side streets, it's just

        me now and the

black night and my

        blue breath and the

fresh flakes falling

        past the glowing

domes of streetlamps.

II.

worlds/within/the words

Eradication: pulling up by the roots
(Radical Fairy Tale #1)

    I. Prologue: before the words

Fairy: fay, one of the Fates
Tale: guile, artifice
Plagiarism: a kidnapping

    II. The pre-amble: before the walk

The Auspices: divining omens through bird flight
The Waif: to waver, to shake
Her Subtlety: thinly woven
Her Sanguinity: bloodiness, ruddiness
Her Cap: a hooded cloak
Her Caprice: a shivering

    III. The Plot: a land marker, a boundary point

The Path: to go forward
The Aquiescence: to yield quietly
The Adolescence: to be kindled, to burn
The Prevarication: to walk crookedly
The Delirium: to turn the furrow against the grain
The Elimination: to cross a boundary
The Egregiousness: to be cast out of the herd
The Precipitation: to hurl downward, as off a great cliff

    *****

Oh, the Wilds: shaggy haired, wooly
Oh, the Marigolds: the Virgin Mary, the riches
Oh, the Wolf, The Lupine: (origin uncertain)
Oh, the Desire: to await from the stars
Oh, the Ravenousness: to snatch, to seize

    *****

The Muscles: mouse-like
The Drowning: to become drunk
The Superfluity: to overflow

The Lunacy: the moon
The Period: a cycle

      *****

The Hunter: one who seizes by the hand
The Escape: to remove one's cape
The Rifle: to scrape, to scratch, to heckle
The Embarassment: to block, impede

    IV. The Denoument: to tie up

The Result: to rebound, to spring back
The Aplomb: to gain equilibrium, perpendicularity
The Destination: to fasten, to secure
The Home: to lie down, to rest.

Sanitation

> *From the example of the past, the man of the present acts*
> *Prudently so as not to imperil the future.*
> —Titian

Workdays he'd get up in the burnt-toast

darkness, his ragged flannels bearing the stain

Of shame and hangover. He knew his station

Offered no satiation for saint or satan or the nation-

Less tribe of immigrant laborers whose onanist

Rants moaned drunken philosophies into

The echo-y halls of his mind's lonely Stoa.

But I also remember the odd sober stint

Of first light mornings, how after he'd drink his instant

coffee, he'd pour us each an early morning toast

and we'd clink shot glasses, mine an o.j. bright with sunshine tint.

Zeno's Paradox

I rounded up because I wanted to be old,
And let's face it: 17 and a half is *nearly* 18.
I stopped when I turned 34. My sister
Phoned to say I was middle-aged since
Dad had died at 68: A half-life, my life

Sentence that has stayed with me for seven
And a half years—nearly eight. I'm on 41 now
And heading south, highway 41, that is:
Lake Shore Drive. I know this road well—
the cemetery, the totem pole, the vacant moorings

In the semi-frozen harbor.
This blue-vast sky. I've never looked up
Lapis lazuli. As I reach the S-Curve,
Lake waves slap and leap over the stone slabs
Of the guard wall beyond The Drake.
Another wall my father helped build.

Adult Literacy

The grip told plenty:
clenched fists held too far away
From the ink, the lead, the wax
(Some still used crayon). Most
Held their pens like knives slashing
The blades toward themselves,
Like anxious children ripping open
Christmas presents sealed
With too much packing tape. When
They could not write their names,
I suggested they draw themselves,
Their homes. Their stick figure
Self-portraits were glass fragile:
Most had eyes, but no mouths, arms
But no hands, unable to grasp
The vacant landscape of an otherwise
Empty page. Their homes were tiny
Boxes with sloped sides—no doors,
No windows, no means of escape.

Haiku (II)

back from Iraq—
my former student
remembers freshman year

after school
the janitor reads the board
before erasing it

Mermaid

The day before we took the plunge we drove to Ocean
City. I'd never tried to swim in anything so vast, but you
were fearless, showing me how to wait for the sea to crest
and break, how to tumble and roll through the great swells,
senseless, salt-stung and blind without my glasses I'd left
on our beach towel, deaf above the water roar, kissing you
at the sand bar, while mad waves crashed all around us. How
like a mermaid you swam, how beautiful every time you
surfaced, shimmered, how ready: remember? How ready we
were to take each other's hands and dive together somewhere.

Goldfish

No one remembers the names of the goldfish
We buried in the backyard, but
In the summer, when I push the mower around
The smooth circle of river stones where they lie,
I remember the cool puddle of our shadows,
How my son and I held hands as we walked inside,
How after our moment of silence, no one said anything.

Tomcat

We knew right
    away the young tomcat
        we took from the shelter
Would be a good
    hunter: the way he raked
        his claws over the new armoire,
The way he slashed
    his kitten paws, like tiny
        scimitars, at children running past.
One morning
    I saw him lying
        on his back in the basement
Skewering a mouse
    in mid-air as if he were
        playing catch with a plush toy.
When the weather
    warmed, I saw him
        crouched under a bird feeder
In my neighbor's yard
    waiting like a mortician
        in the shade of a honey locust.

Motley

Our dog had long hair and he seemed to shed his coat all year round. Every time we swept we gathered huge dustpan-fuls of hair and made the same joke: "There's enough fur here for another dog." He was a good dog with deep, expressive eyes like Buster Keaton. He lived a full life—puppy craziness modulating into mellowness, before sleep overtook him. We missed him terribly. And then one day, when we came downstairs to drink our coffee, work on our puzzles, and trade stories of newspaper villains, who should come trotting in but that other dog. He seemed to float as much as gallop, as if he were made only of fur—no blood, no bones. Except the fur didn't match. It was all different colors and textures, like he was cobbled together from a remnants bin. No doubt about it he was motley. Motley turned out to be made up of all the dogs we've ever known—Lucy and Red and Lance—yes, and even dogs from childhood. He brought us the outside world: wet leaves; the hum of the mailman's truck; flowers withering, blossoming; a baby stroller's squeaky wheel. Everywhere we went, Motley followed with an easy neutrality. And at night, he curled up at our feet, content with all the ground he covered, discovered, and he made us so happy by reminding us we had shared so many lives together.

Hunky Dory: Cento

(from David Bowie's Hunky Dory)

The key to the city?

Flashing teeth of brass

Like the crust of the sun.

Don't deceive with belief.

Take the car downtown.

Be a standing cinema—

A tactful cactus,

A crack in the sky.

I think about the world

To come: I'm living

In a silent film.

I'm not a prophet,

Or a stone age man,

But just remember—

Happiness is happening.

Fear is in your head,

Only in your head.

Don't kid yourself:

The days? They belong to you.

After Thought Autumn

Hymns be damned, autumn: your legacy hedges
on your after-glow frippery. Sit and stay a spell.
What else hangs in your fiery armoire, your grim
grimoire? Say a spell. *Mirabile dictu*: Sugar maples
simmer and stew in tandoori hues: cinnamon, curry,
cayenne, clove. Indian summer. The morning air
tenses: What will you have been? Are you killing
time by leafing through a magazine called *Ardency*?
Are you a wish, a wick? A wood pile of linger sticks
around a cone of campfire kindling? Will you? Kill
you? Maybe, like a Michaelmas daisy, blooms and
bruises, waits for must—a gust of rusty reminder.
Wither art, winter, whither? You're still throwing
shade at the dusky husks while every *yet* whets our
appetites: sins, sings, sinks. Then again, yet again,
wet again, until the first frisk of winter's whisker.

III.

worlds/inside/the world

Production Notes for *February: The Movie*

1. Snow covers everything like a film.

2. The only theatre in town is showing *The Return of the Bride of Quietness*.

3. Overhead, a wedge of geese: A greater than sign? Lesser than? A boomerang?

4. The world is as quiet, white, and immobile as a crime scene. *Go back to your homes. There is nothing more to see.*

5. We are living in an ice pick epoch.

6. You are between stations now, and the radio is all snow—static, stasis, metastasis.

7. A two-page spread for glow-in-the-dark, faux snow by Hasbro.

8. As far as the eye can see: pine trees, pining.

9. I.V. tubes hanging from the icy branches.

10. Outside the elementary school, a family of snow people.

11. Paper snowflakes in every classroom window. Some are clearly identical.

12. Children dancing in the grooves of the snow plow.

13. The ground is hard and cold, like Belmondo in *Breathless*.

14. The only diegetic music: the hectic commotion of thick flakes.

15. Snowy mounds: kyphotic, erotic, necrotic.

16. Between the quilts and covers: quivers.

17. Snow covers our footprints before we can make fresh tracks.

18. What made you ever think you could ice skate?

19. Chap stick syllogism: Therefore, all good things must come to an end.

20. Our only aspiration: suspiration

21. Outside the ticket booth, we huddle together for warmth.

22. It's bitter cold, but at least outside we can still see our breath in front of us.

23. The audience sits, facing the white screen in the early dark, waiting for the lights to come on.

24. The cold bothers you more these days.

25. You find you've started to use the word "marrow."

26. A warm memory of Tweety Bird: *I thawed I thaw…*

27. The ice begins to give—a tickle, a trickle, a rivulet.

28. The slow dissolve.

(29. Look before you).

Hopscotch

> *"Explanation is a well-dressed error"*
> —Cortázar, *Hopscotch*

How do you make butterscotch?

One day I vow to read Márquez

in the Plaza Central of Bogotá.

Jojoba for 3rd degree sunburns! I suffer

from a sort of existential mayonnaise.

When has my phone last rung? Ladder

secured, I climb. This 2nd floor altitude

is positively Andean. How do I know that

handyman in Spanish is *un hombre hábil?*

Sparrows are nesting underneath my air

conditioner, pecking out the putty

seal. Acrobatics, circus tricks. I say

Turn it on full blast! Let the sky blue

Wind blow your dandelion fluff where

it will. Let your mind go to seed.

Carnival

the lion tamer's ravaged
with savage scratches
like he's just walked
blind and naked
through a patch of cactus

the fire swallower's voice
is raspy and fractious
can you imagine how he sounded
on the first day of practice?

the tightrope walker's
cracked and chalky toes
inch along the wire
in a death grip hold

she empties her mind
but never forgets:
the love of the crowd
is her safety net

fun house mirrors help us see
the real horror show is normalcy
so now let's take a peek
inside the "Festival of Freaks":

There's a strongman in a singlet
with a dwarf upon his back;
a charmer in a turban
saves us all from snake attack;
and here's The Human Pretzel
with her legs tied round her back

there's an illustrated man
lurking 'round his inky lair—
and a lady combing out
all her unwanted facial hair

the fortune teller's crystal

ball's alive with marble swirl:
a vortex of predictions
from forgotten worlds

and when at last they strike
their sets, pull down their tents, depart
I pour out the contents
of my sawdust heart

All that's left now
of that magic caravan
is the oily rainbow puddle
where the carnival ran

Untidaled

Dawn: the lake wears a suit of lights.

    ***

I hunt for mermaid tears: sea glass.

    ***

Fragments: water-polished, worry-worn, the size of prayer beads.

    ***

For me the sea is Lake Michigan.

    ***

The oceanographer settled our bar bet this way: "Look, Lake Michigan is affected by tides, but the tides are nearly imperceptible, just a few centimeters per year, easily masked, for example, by changes in barometric pressure. So, you'd be just as right calling the Lake tidaled as you would untidaled."

    ***

Wait till the waves get wind
of that little nugget!

    ***

I glass the shore with finger goggles.

    ***

I'm trying to get a handle on light and shade.

    ***

Translucence isn't nuisance

to the color
blind.

***

Greens and reds blend into the backwashed backdrop.

***

Amber? Warmer!

***

White pieces like soap flakes, like baby teeth.

***

Transparency is my specialty.

***

Clear pieces jut out in relief—
gargoyles on a Gothic cathedral.

***

The glass smooth water marbles the shallows.

***

The lake is a mirror.
(All that sand, I guess).

***

I am here and there.

***

Midlife is inside me.

***

Gull cry: *debris, skree…debris, skree…*

***

Memory: that last holiday in Chicago. We drive to the lake and hoist Mom in her wheelchair litter to the edge of the shore. She digs her feet in the sand and listens to the lapping water. How young she looks, a *colleen* reclining on the rocks at Ballybunion, the wind toying with her wild curls like wisps of dune grass.

***

It was Easter,
No: Thanksgiving, yes,
I'm sure it was Easter.

***

It all comes back.
The turbid ebb and flow.

***

The echolalia of plangency.

***

The relentless, hell-bent-ness of purpose.

***

Only sound
Waves.

***

I am surrounded by clocks.

Time

  The year my voice broke I walked around the neighborhood, trying it on for size. I spoke in deep, rich tones, like a news anchor, asking every woman I'd pass, "Excuse me, ma'am, but do you have the time?" Or to men: "Hey, man, what time you got?"

  The word *man*, like the word *cool*, takes a lot of practice to say naturally.

  After school, I'd head to my shift at McDonald's, hopping on a CTA bus and asking the driver, "Hey, man, what time you got?" And when the driver'd hold out his large wrist with the huge clock face smiling in a nest of forearm hair, I'd say, "Cool," almost-ing that last letter, swallowing it so that it sounded like a "coo." Then I'd take my seat with the other men on their way to or from work.

Midlife

              if   [the]

      idl   e

      id

      'd

      di   e   [inside]

m   e

Night Meds

Our breath is plastic, elastic,
                                      extended-
Release and capsule-plaited.
Our hearts and minds
And moods are regulated.

Our lips, too, bear residue.
But our tongues taste true.

Assisted Living

this is her world now
this snow globe world
her cloudy eyes staring
past the white hospital
curtain of snowflakes
scattering like ashes
my mother is she
as afraid as I am?

plenty of winter
left the orderly says
examining her liver
spots a tangle
of rosary beads
dangling from her
hands as he Velcros
the blood pressure cuff
squeezes releases
listening to her
inaudible heartbeat

*

Last night I had the dream again:
I'm a young child. My aged parents,
Prematurely grey in hospital gowns are
The strongest man and woman in the world.

Cartoon strongmen—
Spinning medicine balls on
Fingertips, doing sets of curls with
Barbells the size of Buicks, flossing
Their dentures with snarls of barbed wire.

I am on a rickety school bus, the last child
To be dropped off, and when I reach
My stop, what I think is the end of my block,
I have to avoid a minefield of smoking, fiery
Craters: where my parents have stepped

I cannot follow in their footsteps,
So I hop from foot to foot, leaping over
Lava puddles while they watch me
From the curbside, mindlessly flexing.

I never make it home.

*

later we join the others
in the community room
nothing stirs
the brakes are on
every wheelchair
no fresh air we stare
at the big screen TV
unscrambling static
until we are absorbed
by the purple glow
all of us the color of twilight.

A Young Poet Responds to a Poem by Robert Bly

I wish I could write a poem about the self-
Satisfied, one-legged heron, un-moving
But for a quick sip in a glassy lake,
No need for motion, no desire for flight,
Or perhaps a squid, tentacles a-tangle,
Floating mindlessly in the blind ocean…

But, seriously, what has the heron written
With all those quills? What has the squid
Ever penned with all that goddamned ink?

Ode to Vivian Maier

1.

Mercurial, this mirror magic

mostly self-taught, self-caught

street witness, a crystal ball

between her legs, her likeness, like

she's giving birth to her-

                      self-

                                  portrait.

2.

Here's one: department store window

shoppers, all of us, in a hall of glass

and shadow: Now you see her,

now you don't. She's everywhere

and nowhere… an image, breathing

in the air of others and otherness.

There she is again: upside down

inside the cigarette dispenser,

in the industrial fan, at a cozy table

for two (make that three), a shy

couple caught in the folds of her housecoat.

3.

She's a gumshoe sleuth, a detective

of perspective on the trail, on the move,

her evidence evolving in the slimy tray

of stop bath. You'll see that dame's shadow

through the frosted glass before you see her.

4.

Shadows on a cave wall: a high heeled shoe,

a handbag, a garbage can in a blind alley.

Or, shadows on a wave call:

in this one a horseshoe crab

over her shadow heart, its tail

pointing to a piece of driftwood,

with a rusted nail driven through:

the residue of someone else's crucifixion.

5.

Oh, Vivian, your fixation with your shadow

self—your nanny props: the bicycle,

the carpet bag, the sunhat, the umbrella,

ready for any contingency to countenance

a snarling cat, your penumbra on the patina

of a silver platter, a shiny hub cap nabbed

in the glint of chrome, a rear-view mirror,

a yard sale sign, running your length-

wise shadows, against the wash of Lake Mich.

beaches and night-stand leavings, books,

teacups, curios, a field of buttercups, finding

light even in street litter by shoplifting

the sheen from beauty parlor windows.

Haiku III

storm windows
rattling
in the nursery

                                Christmas morning
                                my daughter trying to live
                                in the present

electrical storm …
my daughter practices
the letter "S"

Reflection

Like Echo, my autistic daughter learned to speak
By repeating speeches she heard or read in books.

Like Narcissus, I turned inward, finding identical
Symptoms in my own behavior: my imperfect eye-contact,

My uncanny recall of phone numbers from earlier lives. Why
Couldn't I see the signs any earlier? Why did I,

Like Narcissus, put a pretty face on it? When she'd spin
In circles for hours at a time, I joked she might work for NASA

One day. When she learned to read earlier than other kids,
Spending entire days staring at books

I thought this reflected well on me. But, she is not Echo, and
I am not Narcissus—even if we are not yet out of the woods.

And I have never loved anyone so much. Not even myself.

Communication Disorder: Blanche

What if I'm not autistic? my autistic daughter asks me
for the three thousandth time today. She's trying
to provoke a response with that line. Again. But she's
staring in a mirror as she says it, and I'm trying to
concentrate on my school papers. It's not easy to help
young writers cultivate their voice, take chances, break
new ground, so I don't even make eye contact. I just say
"But you *are*, Blanche." My daughter is not named Blanche.
It's a reference to the movie *Whatever Happened to Baby
Jane?* a movie she knows nearly by heart about a woman
stuck in the past, lost in the old scripts she performed
as a child actor and my daughter knows the next line "And
tell me what are these awful things I'm supposed to be
doing to you?" but instead she says *Yeah, but what if I'm not?*

Communication Disorder: Forcefield

so we're driving toward the Verizon store my daughter and I to pick up a new phone case since hers though indestructible has been destroyed and she says *I wish I lived with a forcefield around me at all times* and I ignore her since I mean there's a time and a place and it's raining and her cell phone is everything her means of speaking to the world and following world events and taking pictures of her world our world the world and there is a parking place and the rain picks up and I'm wondering about our coverage when she says *then I could walk around and enjoy the grey* and I say listen when we get inside the store let me talk to the salesman because you know what these salesmen are like they're all upsell and bundle packages and we only want one thing and as we race for the door she says *in the silver Miyazaki rain*

Pinners

"You're all gray," my wife said, running her fingers through my hair. She laughed when she said it and I know she said it with love, but I mock-winced, and clutched my heart: "Ouch." I knew I had *some* gray in my hair but she said, "You're all gray," and I started to think she was on to something. It's not just my hair. Maybe I have lost my bounce. My skin has become paler, shiny and veiny, my body rounder and ever more hairless. *I've* become gray, I thought, looking in the mirror the next day, gray and rotund, like those rubber balls we used to play Pinners against the front steps of our houses.

On every bungalow, even the ones with wooden stairs, the bottom step was always a cement slab, so we'd throw the ball against that bottom step using baseball rules. Sometimes the ball would just carom weakly off the step and dribble down the walk. You'd gobble it up. Routine out. But if you bobbled the grounder (E-1), or if the ball somehow squirted through to the sidewalk, man on first. The parkway grass was a two-bagger, a triple if it reached the street, and every now and then—when you hit the intersection of the x- and y-axes of that bottom step, the magical inflection point of the rise and glide- that ball would travel clear over to the other side of the street (where there was probably another game of Pinners going on) and then, in your best announcer voice you'd scream, "Hey, hey!" or "Holy Cow" or "You can put it on the board" before cutting a quick jazz square, tagging all the bases and stomping on home. You might even step out, take a bow, and tip your obligatory snap-back to the adoring crowd, (because gods really do answer fan mail), before returning to the shadowland of the dugout.

A Walk in the Woods with My Daughter

I wish I could pocket the sage
and sawdust, the moss and purple
honeysuckle from our walk
in the woods tonight, the way
our dogs carry the diary of their day's
journey in the flare of their nostrils,
on the tips of their tongues, on the pads
of their feet. Is that why they curl
up like question marks at night:
to surround themselves with
the sense of where they've been?

Acknowledgments

I am grateful to the many editors who have read and encouraged my work along the way. In particular, I'd like the thank the editors of the following journals in which these poems first appeared:

After Hours: "On Top of the World, Photograph of My Father" (also appeared in the anthology *No Tender Fences: An Anthology of Immigrant and First-Generation American Poetry*)

Anthropology and Humanism: "Sun Poisoning"

Bennington Review: "Blanche" and "Forcefield"

Blue Lake Review: "Dipso Facto"

The Cortland Review: "Goldfish"

The Ekphrastic Review: "Ode to Vivian Maier"

The Golden Shovel Anthology: "Immigrant" (also in the anthology *No Tender Fences*)

Great Lakes Review: "Untidaled"

Journal of Language and Literacy Education: "Adult Literacy"

Peauxdunque Review: "A Walk in the Woods with My Daughter"

Poetry East: "Halfway Up the Stairs"

North Chicago Review: "A Young Poet Responds to Robert Bly"

Rhino: "Eradication (Radical Fairy Tale #1)"

River Oak Review: "Production Notes for *February: The Movie*"

Rooting (Finishing Line Press): "Sweetness"; "Skitching"

Sport Literate: "Pinners"

Third Wednesday: "Streets and San" and "After Thought Autumn"

The Willow Review: "Refrain" and "Reflection"

Wordplaygrounds: "Names" (first appeared in *Wordplaygrounds,* NCTE Press)

The haiku first appeared in ***The Heron's Nest; Modern Haiku;*** and ***Frogpond.***

Notes

"Immigrant" is based on the poem "Subway," by Carl Sandberg

"intervention" is for Mike, one of the bravest men I've ever known

"Sanitation" is based on the anagram poems in Terrance Hayes' *Hip Logic*

"Hunky Dory" and "Mermaid" are especially for Eleni

John S. O'Connor is a public school teacher and a writer from Chicago. Previous books include two books on the teaching of writing (*Wordplaygrounds*; and *This Time It's Personal*) a chapbook of poems called *Rooting*; and three books of haiku, most recently *Natural Consequences*, a winner of the annual Brooks Books chapbook contest. His poems have appeared in places such as *Bennington Review, The Cortland Review, Poetry East* and *Rhino*.

www.ingramcontent.com/pod-product-compliance
Lightning Source LLC
Chambersburg PA
CBHW030056170426
43197CB00010B/1553